Arba Lankton

Thoughts on Religion and Temperance

Arba Lankton

Thoughts on Religion and Temperance

ISBN/EAN: 9783337877026

Printed in Europe, USA, Canada, Australia, Japan

Cover: Foto ©Lupo / pixelio.de

More available books at **www.hansebooks.com**

THOUGHTS

ON

Religion and Temperance.

BY

ARBA LANKTON.

"I'll preach as though I ne'er should preach again,
And as a dying man, to dying men."

HARTFORD, CT.
PUBLISHED BY ARBA LANKTON.
1872.

STAND FAST.

Watch ye, stand fast in the faith, quit you like men, be strong.—1 *Cor.* 16 : 13.

THE terms in this verse are all military. "Watch ye!" watch and be always on your guard, lest you be surprised by your enemies. Keep your scouts out, and all your sentinels at their posts, lest your enemies steal a march upon you. See that the place you are in be properly defended, and that each be alert to perform his duty.

1st. Watch ye, that your mind be always stayed on God. The devil and his instruments may do strange things to support the credit of his falling cause, and lying wonders may be wrought, that may stagger the incautious; but whatever would draw us from Christ must be rejected with abhorrence.

We are too apt to look upon outward grandeur with the eye of sense, and to be influenced by the pomp and glory of the world, and forgetting the requirement of God, laid down in his holy word, telling us to "watch and pray lest we enter into temptation," we lean to our own understanding instead of trusting in God, and the result is that our courage and strength fail us in the hour of trial, as they did Elijah the prophet, at one time, when the wicked queen of Israel threatened to take away his life. Instead of magnifying his office, he in effect rejected it. Like Jonah, he fled from the presence of the Lord, and lay concealed in Horeb, when he ought to have confronted the idolatrous Jezebel, and endeavored to confirm the convictions which the late miracle had made on the minds of the people. He betrayed an unworthy fear of

A

man, or rather of a foolish woman, and seems to have lost his confidence in God.

With undaunted courage he had lately reproved King Ahab, and confounded all the priests of Baal; yet now he is frightened by a passionate queen, and runs away to Horeb. Let us be profited by Elijah's experience, and watch, that our minds be always stayed on God; trusting in his written promise, which says, "Wait on the Lord; be of good courage, and he shall strengthen thine heart." Ps. 27 : 14.

2nd. Watch ye; against evil, internal and external. A person once came to Christ, and offered himself to become one of his disciples, and only begged that he might first bid adieu to his friends, and settle his worldly affairs. But Christ seeing that his heart was entangled with worldly things, let him know the impossibility of uniting the services of God and mammon. "No man having put his hand to the plough, and looking back, is fit for the kingdom of God." While he hankers after the world, and parts from it with reluctance, he will not heartily discharge the duties of a faithful Christian. Worldly pursuits may prove a dangerous snare to draw off the heart from Christ; even those that we may lawfully mind, are apt to engage unlawful and inordinate affections after them, When once we have set our faces heavenward, let us *never look back*, but "remember Lot's wife." Coke's Com., 3d vol., 546 p.

The Scriptures teach us to "keep our hearts with all diligence, for out of the heart are the issues of life." Our Saviour taught his disciples that "Out of the heart proceed evil thoughts, murders, adulteries, fornications, thefts, false witness, and blasphemies;" these, said Christ, "are they which defile a man." Matt. 15: 19, 20.

We should come to the great physician, even Christ, by

faith and prayer, and have our hearts healed of the plague of sin; then watch against sin, and never harbor sinful thoughts, or wicked desires in our hearts, not even for a moment, no more than we would hold our hand in the fire, and not expect to be burned; for if sinful thoughts and wicked desires are permitted to dwell in the heart, they will most surely burst forth in wicked words and wicked actions.

How important that we take heed to the directions given us by Paul, to "be sober and vigilant, for our adversary—the devil—goeth about as a roaring lion, seeking whom he may devour."

3rd. Watch ye. to receive good. We are commanded to "grow in grace and in the knowledge of our Lord and Saviour, Jesus Christ," and we may do this, by diligently improving the various means of grace which God has instituted. Among these are the private duties of the closet, prayer, reading God's holy word, and meditation. We may receive good by attending the public ordinances of God's house, the preaching of his word, the prayer meetings and the sacrament of the Lord's Supper. And as we have opportunity it is our duty to watch and improve these privileges. so that they shall not arise up against us at the day of judgment.

My brethren, when in secret you pray, watch ye, and pray to your Father who seeth in secret, expecting that, according to his promise, he "*will* reward you openly." And be watchful, if in the house of God, that you do not content yourselves with the means, without the end, lest the fowls should come down, and devour the sacrifice which was prepared for God, and the enemy take away the seed which was sown in the heart.

4th. Watch ye to *do good.* The Bible tells us, "He that knoweth to do good, and doeth it not, to him it is sin." Also, "Let your light so shine before men, that they may see your good works, and glorify your Father which is in heaven." We may do much good to others, by always being steadfast in well-doing ourselves. Mankind are naturally very imitative; and thousands have been influenced to try to live the lives of the righteous, by the good example of others. There is a good done of which we can never tell the when or where. "Remember the power of indirect influences, those which distil from a life, not from a sudden brilliant effort. The former never fail, the latter often."

It is said of Rev. Dr. Wilbur Fisk, that "it was his rare moral character, more than his intellectual eminence, that gave him such magic influence over other minds. All about him felt a sort of self-respect in respecting him."

We may do much good by visiting the sick, and relieving their wants, so far as we are able. We may go to the bedside of some poor sinner, who has lived in rebellion against God, and now he feels that he is going to die, and is about to meet his offended Maker face to face. He cannot escape, and as he thinks of his past wicked life, and remembers that the Bible has said, "The wicked shall be turned into hell, with all nations that forget God," he fears the consequence of his sins, and cries out like the Philippian jailor of old, "Sirs, what must I do to be saved?" The visitor can then tell the sick man, to "Believe on the Lord Jesus Christ and thou shalt be saved;" and then instruct him, and pray for him, and God in answer to prayer, will save the sinner, if he heartily repents of his sins, and seeks for pardon through the merits of Christ.

We may visit the Christian who is sick, and tell him that these light afflictions, though for the present they

Sirs: What Must I Do to be Saved?

may seem grievous, yet if he is only faithful until death, "they shall work out for him a far more exceeding and eternal weight of glory;" and the sick pilgrim may take fresh courage, and pass triumphantly over the river Jordan into the haven of rest.

5th. We should watch over each other. By observing others, we may see wherein they err, and kindly tell them, when we are alone with them, and so help them to do better. They may see faults in us, and tell us of them, and "a word fitly spoken is like apples of gold in pictures of silver." "How good it is to know that ever amid the world's cold selfishness, there are warm and loving hearts beating for us, a spirit of kindness brooding o'er us; the thought, bright and beautiful, flitting at times like some gay dream across our pathway, gives us fresh courage, and a stronger purpose to the soul in the fierce conflict of life's great battle.

Stand fast in the faith. First. In the true theory thereof. Second. In the practice of the true theory of faith.

1. In the true theory of the faith. There are many theories, and we should find the right one and stand fast in that. The Mormons believe in Christ, but they license polygamy and other things contrary to the gospel theory of faith in Christ, by which salvation to the soul is secured. The Roman Catholics believe in Christ, but allow things contrary to the gospel theory, and hence Romanism is not the true theory.

But the true theory of the faith is, to believe in Christ both as a vicarious and also as a propitiatory sacrifice. The word vicarious means, "substituted in the place of another." Christ offered himself and died on the cross for our sins; that whosoever believeth on him might not perish but have everlasting life. Thereby he became a

PRAY FOR HIM. *Page* 8.

vicarious sacrifice for sinful man. Christ was also a propitiatory sacrifice, that is, accepted of God for man, and God was reconciled to save men if they would believe on him whom he had sent. And that God accepted of Christ, is shown in Matt. 3: 17, "And lo! a voice from heaven saying, This is my beloved son, in whom I am well pleased."

We must stand fast in this faith, holding fast what we have already received as the truth of God; for it is the gospel by which ye shall be saved, and by which ye are now put in a state of salvation.

2. We should stand fast in the practice of the true faith. No matter how many errors may be cherished in the hearts of those around us; we, like good soldiers of the Lord Jesus Christ, should manfully "fight the good fight of faith." being "steadfast, unmovable, always abounding in the work of the Lord, forasmuch as ye know that your labor is not in vain in the Lord."

"Quit you like men."

1. Do not act as mere animals, who have nothing to live for but sensual pleasures, Man has faculties and powers which raise him in the scale of creation far above every other living thing with which we are acquainted. Man has reason, the noblest of all his attributes, and which has been denied to the brute creation. Animals are guided in supplying their wants by instinct; but man not only has instinct, but reasoning powers, by which he is able to think, study, and understand right from wrong, to learn who made him, and for what purpose he was made, and man with his superior knowledge is permitted to have dominion over the brute creation.

2. Do not live as mere children, tossed to and fro by every wind of doctrine, but let your understanding receive the truth; let your judgment determine on the

absolute necessity of retaining it, and give up life, rather than give up the testimony of God.

3. "Stand fast, quit you like men," capable through the grace of God assisting you, of performing what you undertake to do; and when you are attacked by the enemy of truth, and he tries to get you to give up your faith in Christ, do not shrink or yield for one moment, remembering the Scotch general's speech to his army on one occasion, just before they were to attack an enemy, "Scotchmen," said he, "there are your enemies out there, you must conquer them, or they will conquer you." And it is just so with us, we must, with God's help, overcome our human and spiritual foes, or they will conquer us.

Finally, brethren, "be strong." Put forth all the vigor and energy which God has given you, in maintaining and propagating the truth, and your spiritual strength will increase. God will help you if you are willing to help yourselves. Remember, "your cause is good; it is the faith, the religion of Jesus. He is your

captain in the field; and should you even die in the contest, the victory is yours."

"So when this corruptible shall have put on incorruption, and this mortal shall have put on immortality, then shall be brought to pass the saying that is written, Death is swallowed up in victory."

"O death, where is thy sting? O grave where is thy victory?"

"The sting of death is sin; and the strength of sin is the law."

"But thanks be to God, which giveth us the victory through our Lord Jesus Christ."

"Therefore, my beloved brethren, be ye steadfast, unmovable, always abounding in the work of the Lord, forasmuch as ye know that your labor is not in vain in the Lord." 1 Cor. 15: 54–58.

FIRMNESS.

"Be firm. The wind and the waves may beat against a rock standing in a troubled sea; but it remains unmoved. Be you like that rock. Vice may entice, and the song and the cup may invite. Beware! stand firmly at your post. Let your principles shine forth unobscured.

There is glory in the thought that you have resisted temptation, and conquered. Your bright example will be to the world what the lighthouse is to the mariner; it will guide others to the port of virtue and safety."

WHAT THE LIGHTHOUSE IS TO THE MARINER. *Page* 14.

A Prize Fighter Turned Preacher.

THE preacher, Richard Weaver, is thus described in an English newspaper:

"A new preacher, by name Richard Weaver, formerly a prize-fighter and a collier in the North, has appeared in London, and is producing very deep and wide-spread impressions by open-air addresses, on large masses of the population. He was announced first of all by a handbill, to preach and 'sing' at the Cumberland Market. And 'sing' as well as 'preach,' he can do to the melting down of hundreds.

One night, addressing a number of poor men and women on the words, 'They shall return to Zion with songs,' he said: 'I was always fond of singing; I believe I was born to sing; but the songs I used to sing are not the songs I love now.'

'O my dear men, you sing, 'Britons never, never shall be slaves;' but what slaves you are to your own lusts, to the devil, to the landlord!'

'I used to sing, 'We won't go home till morning;' the landlord loves to hear that. I've sung that five nights together, and spent seventy dollars on one spree, and got turned out at the end. But I've learned better songs; I'll tell you some of the songs I love now. Here's one

'O happy day that fixed my choice
On thee, my Saviour and my God.'

And here's another:

'There is a fountain filled with blood,
Drawn from Immanuel's veins.'

The speaker quoted with wonderful rapidity, but without the semblance of irreverence, at least a dozen hymns, or portions of hymns, some of which he sung, the meeting taking up the chorus. Then he related the following anecdote, with a pathos and tenderness of voice and manner which told how affectionate a heart and how delicate a mind may be developed, by the grace of God, in a man employed in the hardest work, and once addicted to the grossest vice.

'I knew a collier in Staffordshire who had one dear little girl, the last of four or five. This child was the light of his eyes, and as he came from the pit at night she used to meet him at the door of his cot to welcome him home. One day when he came in to dinner he missed his little darling, and going into the house with his heavy coal-pit clogs, his wife called him up stairs. The stillness of the place and her quiet voice made his heart sick, and a foreboding of evil came upon him. His wife told him they were going to lose their little lamb; she had had an apoplectic fit, and the doctor said she could not live. As the tears made furrows down his black face, and as he leaned over his dying darling, she said, 'Daddy, sing

'Here is no rest—is no rest!''

'No, my child, I can't sing, I'm choking: I can't sing.' 'O do, daddy, sing 'Here's no rest.'' The poor fellow tried to sing, (*preacher sings*,)

'Here on the earth as a stranger I roam,
Here is no rest—is no rest!'

But his voice could not make way against his trouble. Then he tried again, for he wanted to please his sweet little girl, (*preacher sings*,)

'Here are afflictions and trials severe,
Here is no rest—is no rest!
Here I must part with the friends I hold dear,
Yet I am blest—I am blest!'

Again his voice was choked with weeping, but the little one whispered, 'Come, daddy, sing 'Sweet is thy promise.'' And the poor father goes on again,

'Sweet is thy promise I read in thy word,
Blessed are they who have died in the Lord,
They have been called to receive their reward,
There, there is rest—there is rest!'

'That's it, daddy,' cried the child, 'that's it;' and with her arms round the collier's neck she died happy in the Lord.'

We cannot describe the thrilling effect of Mr. Weaver's singing in the midst of preaching, it is so natural, so free from every thing like premeditation or aiming at effect.

It is said that from forty to fifty persons were hopefully converted by one appeal. One of these cases was that of a careless young sailor, brought to the meeting by his mother, and on this Weaver founded the appeal, 'O mothers, go on praying forever; never mind what they are or where they are; if any prayers reach heaven, a mother's do. Eight years ago the news sounded from heaven to the poor old woman in Shropshire, 'Richard Weaver is born again!'"

THE BIBLE.

"This little book I'd rather own,
Than all the gold and gems
That are in Monarchs' coffers shown,
Than all their diadems.
Nay! were the seas one crysolite,
The earth a golden ball,
And diamonds all the stars of night,
This book, were worth them all."

BE GENTLE TO YOUR WIFE.

Be gentle, for you do not know
How many trials rise;
Although to thee they may be small,
To her of giant size.

Be gentle, though perchance that lip
May speak a murmuring tone;
The heart may beat with kindness yet,
And joy to be thine own.

INVITATION.

INVITATION.

"*Let the wicked forsake his way, and the unrighteous man his thoughts; and let him return unto the Lord, and He will have mercy upon him; and to our God. for He will abundantly pardon.*" *Isaiah* 55: 7.

I. Let us consider who are the wicked and unrighteous. They are those persons who wander away from God, and commit sin by breaking his law. The command of God is, that we have no other gods before Him; that we love Him with all our hearts, and serve Him with all our might; and it seems to me that those persons who love *any* object, whether it be our friends, our own ease, worldly honor, riches or any thing, better than to love and obey God, their righteous Sovereign are both sinful and wicked. Again, we are commanded "not to take the name of God in vain;" and every profane person must be wicked. We are commanded to "Remember the Sabbath day, to keep it holy." Sabbath breakers are wicked. The commandment tells us, "six days shalt thou labor;" and some one has said, that "It is just as bad not to labor the six days, as it is to labor on the Sabbath." We are taught by the Apostle, "*Be not slothful in business,*" but *diligent,* "*fervent in spirit,* serving the Lord." And the slothful in business are wicked. Children are commanded to "obey their parents in the Lord," for this is right, and those children who refuse to comply with the command are sinful and wicked, for the apostle has said, that sin is the transgression of the Law, and I might say, that murderers, adulterers, thieves and liars, *all* who break either one or all the laws of God, are in his sight, both sinful and wicked. Sin is the same in essence, in the boy who steals the first cent from his employer's drawer, as it is in the man who plunges the dagger in his neighbor's heart; both might lie and deny their crime; these three sins in their essence are the same.

Illustrations showing who are the wicked.

Our first parents, Adam and Eve, were created in the image of God; and in the last verse of the first chapter of Genesis, we are told, that "God saw every thing that he had made, and behold it was very good." Mankind with the rest are pronounced "very good."

"And the Lord God commanded the man, saying, "*Of every tree of the garden thou mayest freely eat: but of the tree of the knowledge of good and evil, thou shalt not eat of it; for in the day that thou eatest thereof thou shalt surely die.*" But man broke the law by eating of the forbidden fruit, and in breaking the law, he sinned against God, and man became "dead in trespasses and sins," and "so death hath passed upon all men, for that all have sinned."

Death of the body is a separation of the soul from the body, and man separated himself morally speaking, from God, when he broke his law..

And oh, what an awful separation! "It is a separation including on the one hand, the loss of God's favor and delight towards man, and on the other of the loss on their part, of their love and delight towards Him." "It is a separation too, including the loss on their part, of all moral likeness to God, so that they are both guilty and depraved in his sight."

But notwithstanding man has thus wandered, and separated himself from God, by sin, yet this part of the prophecy of Isaiah is full of encouragement to sinners, both Jews and Gentiles to return to God, and be saved."

II. Consider the exhortation found in the text. "Let the wicked forsake his way, and the unrighteous man his thoughts, and let him return to the Lord." This exhortation is a general one, and intended for all nations, both Jews and Gentiles, implying that both had sinned, and lost the favor of God, and were gone astray from him. But God here invites the wicked to forsake his way, and the unrighteous man his thoughts, and to return to God, promising that "he will have mercy and abundantly pardon."

But how are we to return to God?

"Formerly, He was sought in the way of sacrifices, and this was the way that David and others found Him. But all this was only typical of that "new and living way by which we draw near to God," Christ is the way; the only way, "for there is none other name under heaven given among men whereby we must be saved." "In all our seeking unto God, therefore, we must come by faith in the Mediator."

"Jesus, the name to sinners dear,
The name to sinners given,
It scatters all their guilty fear,
It turns their hell to heaven."

"Then let the wicked forsake his way,"—his evil or wicked way; his sinful course or manner, called his way, as being natural, customary, and dear to him, and in opposition to God's good way.

"Let the wicked forsake his way, and the unrighteous man his thoughts;" the sinful desires and purposes of the heart, and thus he strikes at the root of all sinful actions, and shows that the heart must be changed, as well as the outward conduct.

"Let the wicked forsake his way, and the unrighteous

man his thoughts, and let him return to the Lord." As he departed from God by sin, so let him return to God, by sincere repentance, and faith in the atoning merits of Christ, which will be productive of new obedience to the law of God. He will "cease to do evil and learn to do well."

III. Let us now consider the happy result, if the exhortation is complied with, or the sad result if it is rejected.

If it is complied with and the wicked does forsake his wicked way, and his unrighteous thoughts, and if he will return to the Lord, God has promised that he will have mercy, and he will abundantly pardon. Glory be to God for such a precious promise. Y'es, my readers, though your sins be as scarlet, they may be as white as snow, though they be red like crimson, comply with the terms of salvation, and you shall find that God will have mercy, and he will abundantly pardon. "For God so loved the world, that he gave his only begotten Son, that whosoever believeth on him, might not perish, but have everlasting life."

But, if you reject God's offers of mercy, and wickedly refuse to have Christ Jesus to reign over you here, then at the judgment day, Christ will refuse to own you as one of his disciples, but will say: "Depart from me, ye cursed, into everlasting fire, prepared for the devil and his angels." "And these shall go away into everlasting punishment; but the righteous into life eternal." In the prophecy of Isaiah, it reads, "Say ye to the righteous that it shall be well with him, for they shall eat the fruit of their doings. Wo unto the wicked! it shall be ill with him; for the reward of his hands shall be given him." And our Saviour taught when on earth, that "whosoever forsaketh father or mother or lands, for my sake, and the gospel's," should "receive an hundred fold in this life, with persecutions, and in the world to come eternal life." The Bible tells us, "Surely I know, that it shall be well with them that fear God, which fear before him: but it shall not be well with the wicked," and the Bible contains many illustrations, showing that it has been, and still shall be, well with the righteous, but ill with the wicked. It was well with Adam and Eve in the garden before they had sinned and broken God's law. It was well with righteous Abel, but ill with wicked Cain. It was well with righteous Noah, but ill with his wicked neighbors, who were drowned in the flood. It was well with righteous Daniel in the lions' den, and it was well with the Hebrew children in the fiery furnace, but it was ill with their wicked enemies, who tried to kill them because they strove to fear and obey God.

When a part of the children of Israel forsook the commandments of the Lord, and followed the idol Baal, it went ill with them, for they did not have rain for years, and a great famine spread all over the land; but when the Israelites returned to the true God, He had mercy on them and gave them rain.

"But he that doeth wrong shall receive for the wrong that he hath done, and there is no respect of persons." Col. 3: 25. And I can testify from my own experience, that when I have wandered away from God by sin, and neglected for a season to comply with the divine requirements, then it has been ill with me. But the Holy Spirit, as I trust, suggested this text of Scripture: "Let the wicked forsake his way, and the unrighteous man his thoughts, and let him return unto the Lord, and he will have mercy upon him, and to our God, for he will abundantly pardon," and I fell upon my knees, confessed my sins, and I tried to return to God, pleading his promise, and the merits of Christ, His Son; and I asked forgiveness for his Son's sake. God heard my prayer. He *did* have mercy, and abundantly pardoned. Glory be to God forever.

"Then will I tell to sinners round,
What a dear Saviour I have found;
I'll point to His redeeming blood,
And say, behold the way to God."

And to those who are now wandering away from God, and refusing to obey Him, the sixth and seventh verses of the 55th chapter of Isaiah are most kindly, yet warningly addressed, "Seek ye the Lord while he may be found, call ye upon Him while he is near .Let the wicked forsake his way, and the unrighteous man his thoughts, and let him return to the Lord, and he will have mercy upon him, and to our God for He will abundantly pardon." For now pardon is offered to those who forsake their wicked ways, and return to God. But the words, "while he may be found," and "while he is near," imply that the time *may* come when those who have refused to comply with the terms of salvation, may cry like the rich man in torments, for mercy, but all in vain. The Lord having gone into the marriage supper, and the door being shut, it *will* be shut forever.

A Psalm of Life.

WHAT THE HEART OF THE YOUNG MAN SAID TO THE PSALMIST.

[H. W. LONGFELLOW.]

Tell me not in mournful numbers,
  "Life is but an empty dream!"
For the soul is dead that slumbers,
  And things are not what they seem.

Life is real! Life is earnest!
  Bnd the grave is not its goal;
"Dust thou art, to dust returnest,"
  Was not spoken of the soul.

Not enjoyment, and not sorrow,
  Is our destined end or way;
But to act, that each to-morrow
  Find us farther than to-day.

Art is long, and Time is fleeting;
  And our hearts, though stout and brave,
Still, like muffled drums, are beating
  Funeral marches to the grave.

In the world's broad field of battle,
  In the bivouac of Life,
Be not like dumb, driven cattle!
  Be a hero in the strife!

Trust no Future, howe'er pleasant!
  Let the dead Past bury its dead!
Act,—act in the living Present!
  Heart within, and God o'erhead!

Lives of great men all remind us
  We can make our lives sublime,
And, departing, leave behind us
  Footprints on the sands of time;

Footprints, that perhaps another,
  Sailing o'er life's solemn main,
A forlorn and shipwrecked brother,
  Seeing, shall take heart again.

Let us, then, be up and doing,
  With a heart for any fate;
Still achieving, still pursuing,
  Learn to labor and to wait.

HALTING.

And Elijah came unto all the people and said How long halt ye between two opinions? if the Lord be God, follow Him, but if Baal, then follow him. 1 Kings 18: 21.

Let us as an introduction to this subject, say a few words about the history of this interesting event. It seems from the reading previous to this text, that Ahab, king of Israel, with four hundred and fifty other men, or false prophets, had left the worship of the true God, and gone to worship the idol Baal, which was the Sun. Jehovah was very angry with the king and the people of Israel, for leaving his worship for that of idolatry, and Elijah, one of the Lord's prophets, said unto king Ahab. "As the Lord God of Israel liveth, before whom I stand, there shall not be dew nor rain these years, but according to my word."

Elijah is now commanded to hide himself, lest Ahab should kill him. Elijah hides himself and remains hid for three years and a half. While many others of the prophets of the Lord are slain, Elijah is hid, and kept alive by the power of God. But at the end of three years and six months, he is commanded by God, to appear before Ahab.

"And it came to pass, when Ahab saw Elijah, that Ahab said unto him, Art thou he that troubleth Israel?" "And Elijah answered, I have not troubled Israel; but *thou*, and *thy father's house*, in that *ye have forsaken the commandments of the Lord*, and thou hast followed Baalim."

And the consequence as we have already seen, of their leaving the worship of God for that of idolatry, was that God shut up the windows of heaven, and there was no rain, and in consequence of there being no rain, there came a great famine, all over the land. Elijah told Ahab to gather the prophets of Baal and the children of Israel unto Mount Carmel. They assemble, and Elijah addresses the people in the language of the text: "How long halt ye between two opinions? if the Lord be God, follow him, but if Baal, then follow him."

Let us now consider what it is to halt between two opinions. In this instance, it was to *omit*, *defer*, or *hesitate* about doing the whole will of God. The people feared the King and Queen, and the false prophets, and as they worshiped the idol Baal, and Baal would allow the people to do as they pleased, they were strongly tempted to serve Baal. But their consciences told them better than to renounce wholly the true God. So they were undecided which they would serve.

III. Let us now notice the sin of halting. The Bible tells us, "He that knoweth to do good, and doeth it not, to him it is sin." Now if God by his Holy Spirit, or in any way, calls us to do any work for Him, and we instead of doing it immediately, delay, on the account of the love of ease, of friends, or the things of this world, we sin against God, for he has commanded us, "whatsoever thy hand findeth to do, do it with thy might, for there is no work nor device, nor knowledge, nor wisdom in the grave, whither thou goest." Eccl. 9:10. Let us then work while the day lasts, knowing that soon the night of death will come, when no man can work.

IV. Let us now consider the folly of halting,—for there is great folly, as well as wickedness in indulging habits of halting, and neglecting our known duties, and especially is this foolish in us, to neglect our souls' salvation. "It is a sad sight to see men so nobly made, with such a lofty destiny before them, with so many high hopes of future good, pursuing the miserable phantoms of this life, and choosing pleasure and sinful mirth, while heaven and immortality should be the objects of their choice. And I presume they will continue in this course of madness until death calls them away to the retributions of Eternity. "As it was in the days of Noah, so shall it be in the coming of the Son of Man." Men will eat and drink, work and play; be sorrowful and merry until the end come, and the wicked shall be destroyed.

And I fear that some will be so attached to their pleasures, that they will continue to sport with judgment, until the power of vengeance shall burst upon them."—*Young Man's Friend*, p. 125. *Serm. on Dangerous Amusements.*

A few years since, I spoke to a young man of my acquaintance, about religion. He acknowledged he ought to attend to the subject; but in a halting manner seemed inclined to delay about it. I asked him if he did not intend to seek religion before he died? He said yes; but he wanted to enjoy life first, then he would seek religion. I told him "delays were dangerous," and we parted. About three or four weeks after our talk together, he went to the Car Factory, to work, and was to all human appearance, doing well, as far as worldly matters were concerned; when suddenly the steam boiler exploded, and this man and twenty-seven others were hurried into eternity, and it was supposed that not one of the number killed was a professor of religion. Truly the way of the transgressor is hard, and the Bible tells us, that "The wicked shall be turned into hell, with all nations that forget God." Psalm 9: 17, and also, "He that being often reproved, hardeneth his neck, shall suddenly be destroyed, and that without remedy." Prov. 29: 1,

In applying this snbject, let me say,

To render acceptable service to God, we must love and

serve Him with our whole hearts. Jesus said, "He that is not with me is against me, and he that gathereth not with me scattereth abroad." The Bible tells us "God is faithful, who will not suffer you to be tempted above that ye are able, but will with the temptation also make a way to escape, that ye may be able to bear it." 1 Cor. 10; 13. If we all are tempted, we should with God's help, give the devil a decided No Sir.

Let us examine ourselves, and see whose service we are now in. If you are not now striving to love the Lord with all your heart, you are not in his service, for the Bible tells us, "His servants ye are, whom ye yield yourselves servants to obey," and if you are not in God's service you must be in the Devil's service; and if you continue thus, against God until death, I can only point you to hell as your future unhappy home. The saying of Christ is, "For what is a man profited if he shall gain the whole world and lose his own soul?" Matt. 16: 26. I once heard or read of a man who fell asleep in his boat which was fastened near the shore. While he was sleeping the boat became unloosed, and drifted down the river. The man continued for a while to sleep, unconscious of his danger. When he did finally awake, he was too near the fall to escape, and passed rapidly on to destruction. So it is with many a sinner asleep in sin. He drifts down the stream of life, and when warned by his friends, he says, "There is no danger for me," until accident or sudden sickness comes and death stares him in the face, then he awakes to his awful condition, out of Christ, and exclaims, "It is too late," and dies. "How long halt ye between two opinions?"

If upon a careful examination of your hearts, you find that you are now striving to love the Lord with all your heart, and your neighbor as yourself, and continue so to do, until death, I can with pleasure, point you to heaven as your future happy home forever. For the promise left to us Christians, servants of Christ, is, "Be thou faithful unto death and I will give thee a crown of life."

I once read an incident, which very strongly illustrates the folly and also the sad consequences of halting and neglecting known duties. The incident is said to have occurred while the French army occupied the city of Moscow. A party of officers and soldiers determined to have military dancing assemblies, and for this purpose chose the deserted palace of a Russian nobleman, in the vault of which a large quantity of powder had been deposited. As the sun went down, they began to assemble. The gayest and noblest of the army were there, and merriment reigned over the crowd. That night the city was burnt. During the dance the fire rapidly approached them; they saw it coming, but felt no fear. At length the building next the one which they occupied was on fire. Coming to the windows, they gazed upon the billows of fire which swept upon their fortress, and then returned to their amusement. Again and again they left their pleasure, to watch the progress of the flames. At length the dance ceased and the necessity of leaving the scene of merriment became apparent to all. They were enveloped in a flood of fire, and gazed on with deep and awful solemnity. At length the fire communicating to their own building, caused them to prepare for flight, when a brave young officer, named Carnot, waved his jeweled glove above his head, and exclaimed, "One dance more, and defiance to the flame." All caught the enthusiasm of the moment, and "One dance more and defiance to the flame," burst from the lips of all. The dance commenced, louder and louder grew the sound of music, and faster and faster fell the pattering footsteps of dancing men and women, when suddenly they heard a cry, "The fire has reached the magazine! fly! fly! for life!" One moment they stood, transfixed with horror; they did not know the magazine was there, and ere they recovered from their stupor, the vault exploded, the building was shattered to pieces, and the dancers were hurled into a fearful eternity. The Scripture tells us "To day if ye will hear his voice," that is, God's voice, "harden not your hearts," and I would say in the language of the poet,

"Behold a stranger at the door,
He gently knocks, has knocked before:
Has waited long, is waiting still,
You treat no other friend so ill.

Rise, filled with gratitude divine,
Turn out his enemy and thine,
That soul-destroying monster, sin,
And let the heavenly stranger in.

Admit him, lest his anger burn,
His feet departed, near return,
Admit him, for the hour's at hand,
You'll at his door rejected stand."

Idleness Leads to Want.

SLOTHFULNESS.

Slothfulness consists in "being idle, or unemployed; in a state of inactivity," or in neglecting to perform the work which God by his providence calls us to perform.

It is not always necessary to be entirely unemployed in order to be slothful. For a young man may be engaged in reading the newspapers through the day, when he should be studying his lessons, and though he is employed in reading, yet he is slothful, because he neglects his proper business.

A man may be slothful by occupying more time than is necessary, by being slow in doing his work.

If a person allow himself to lie in bed one or two hours in the morning longer than is necessary for health, that person is slothful. One hour occupied in lying in bed every morning after we should be up, will amount to three hundred and sixty-five hours in the course of a year, or fifteen days and five hours in one year, seventy-six days and one hour in five years. The diligent student seizes the morning hours; and while thousands of human beings, "less resolute and diligent, are slumbering, he is pushing rapidly and strongly the great work of his life."

Dr. Doddridge owed the production of his "Family Expositor," and most of his other writings, to his rising at five instead of seven o'clock in the morning. Other men have saved by the habit of early rising, many precious hours, and devoted them to study. These precious hours that may be saved, no person has the right to waste by slothfulness; "nor to sacrifice for the sake of any graceless self-indulgence." He should strive to redeem them; for, in so many redeemed hours he may, with God's help make an impression on the world that will affect the latest ages, and gather for himself glory that will never fade away. The diligent student "labors with his might. Every energy is called to the subject under investigation." "If his thoughts wander for a moment, they are immediately summoned anew, and led on with increased energy and power, until the allotted task is finished, and the mind has triumphed."

The slothful man loses many blessings he might enjoy just as well as not if he would be diligent and try to do what he is able, for himself and others.

We can be slothful in our thoughts. 1st, By not being diligent in thinking, or not thinking to some purpose, or on some good subject. And we can think on subjects foreign to our proper duties, and think on those things that are hurtful to the mind instead of that which tends to profit. 2d, Much misery is caused by habits of slothfulness. "The sluggard desireth and hath nothing, because his hands refuse to labor." "Except a man deny himself, take up his cross and follow Christ," he can not be his disciple. Nothing can be accomplished but by persevering effort. But while the slothful lose so much by negligence, the Bible tells us, "The thoughts of the diligent tend only to plenteousness."

We are admonished to be "not slothful in business," but diligent in business, "fervent in spirit serving the Lord." "Whatsoever thy hand findeth to do, do it with thy might." Here of course we are only allowed to do those things that are in accordance with God's will. "Fear God and keep his commandments, for this is the whole duty of man." For God will bring every work into judgment, "whether it be good, or whether it be evil."

PRAYER FOR ZION.

"*Pray for the peace of Jerusalem; they shall prosper that love thee.*" *Psalm* 122: 6.

Jerusalem was a place of great importance and interest to the children of Israel, because the house of the Lord was there. It was the great seat and center of religion and justice. Thither the different tribes went up to worship the Lord, for there the ordinances of his worship were established. When David said, "pray for the peace of Jerusalem," he may be understood as speaking figuratively, and not only to pray for the protection and prosperity of the city, but also for the enlargement and establishment of God's church.

Pray for the peace of Jerusalem, not for an absence of strife and confusion merely, for that is implied. Nor was it for a mere stagnant or indifferent state, for in stagnant pools of water there may be deadly pestilential gases arising, that would injure and destroy the health of the people. But David desired the protection of God, and the *real prosperity*, both of the *city*, and also of the Church of God.

As applied to ourselves, for what should we pray, if we desire the prosperity of the Church of God at the present time?

In the first place, then, we should pray for the sanctification of the people. David had prayed, "Create within me a clean heart." "The blessing of the Lord is in the house of the righteous: but his curse is in the house of the wicked." Jesus said, "out of the heart proceed evil thoughts." A woman loved jewelry better than to have a sanctified heart. A wicked "Achan" in the camp, caused the loss of many lives.

Secondly, We pray for a spirit of inquiry and solicitude for the salvation of others. When Wesley's heart was warmed with the love of God, he wanted to save others. The primitive Church felt so. A man spent all night in prayer, then went next morning and told another "I am anxious about your soul." The man he spoke to thought if he was anxious about him, he ought to be anxious about himself, and began to pray and was converted. A young lady at a camp meeting, after she was converted at the altar, went back a little way into the congregation and brought her little brother to the altar.

Thirdly, We should pray for a continuance of brotherly love, in the heart. We are commanded to love each other, and we should remember the power of indirect influences.

Fourthly, Pray for the peace of Jerusalem or the Church of God, in that the people may have a faithful attendance on the ordinances of God's house. There is nothing more hurtful to our soul's prosperity, than neglecting the means of grace, and this I have proved by my own experience.

Now look at the exhortation, Pray for the peace or prosperity of Jerusalem, or the Church of God. And this implies a *continuance* in praying, so that it may bring the prosperity we desire.

Notice some of the benefits we receive from praying.

1, Our *hearts are cleansed* as the *result of prayer*. In the 10th chapter of Judges, we have an account of the children of Israel forsaking God to serve idols, of their being sore distressed; they cried unto the Lord, and at first he would not deliver them. They put away the strange gods from among them, and served the Lord: and his soul was grieved for the misery of Israel. In the next chapter we find that a deliverer was raised up and God delivered their enemies into their hands.

2. Another benefit of prayer is, it increases our interest in the object we pray for: i. e., if we want clean hearts, or the mind that was in Jesus, pray, read God's word, and meditate. If we want sinners saved, or the Church to prosper, pray for it.

It is the man who does not go to the closet and pray, that famishes, and it is the one who neglects the prayer-meeting, who has but little interest in the meetings. Another effect of prayer is, we may have an abundance of the Holy Spirit. It may not come in so great a power at first, but the more we pray, the more we shall have, even groaning that cannot be uttered. The reason why we are not more efficient in the service of God is, the want of more of the Holy Spirit.

At the Saybrook camp-meeting, I think it was, but little was accomplished for two days. A man preached on the Holy Spirit, and when that came, then the work of God prospered. Sinners were led to feel and to flock to the altar.

Again, pray, because it secures God's help. Many are the instances of this in God's word. Sampson prayed, when he was thirsty, and God gave him water out of the ass' jaw bone, with which he had slain a thousand Philistines. Judges 15: 15. God's word in our text should afford us encouragement to pray and labor for the Church; for "they shall prosper that love thee."

Peter loved the Church, and though put in prison, yet the Church prayed for him and God heard and delivered him. God has said, "They that honor me I will honor, but they that despise me, shall be lightly esteemed."

CHRISTIAN ZEAL.*

Let him know, that he which converteth the sinner from the error of his way, shall save a soul from death, and shall hide a multitude of sins. *James* 5: 20.

INTRODUCTION.—Has God in mercy provided that fallen, rebellious, wicked man may be saved through repentance, and faith in Christ; and has he condescended to use *man* as an instrument in saving his fellow men? Why then do not professed Christians exert themselves more, that with the help of God they may convert sinners from the error of their way, and save souls from death, and hide a multitude of sins? Alas, how little do we consider the sad and dangerous state of sinners around us. We, who have felt the love of God in our hearts, while they have it not. We see them wandering quite out of the narrow way, into the broad road that leads to destruction, and yet, how few is the number of professed disciples of Christ who seriously and faithfully show sinners their error and danger, and help them with all their might into the way that leads to life. As this work is very important, both as to the glory of God, and the salvation of men, let us consider the nature of this work, and how it is to be performed.

We do not think it necessary, in order to convert sinners from the error of their way, and save souls from death, that every man should turn a public preacher, or that any should go beyond the bounds of their particular calling. This duty is of another nature.

But each Christian should have his heart touched in

---

* Much of this is taken from Baxter's "Saints' Rest."

sympathy for his fellow men, who are still in the broad road to destruction. We should long for their conversion and salvation; and if we anxiously desired their conversion and salvation, it would prompt us to pray and labor for them; and when rightly performed, with God's blessing, our labor is never in vain in the Lord.

Should we be among the ignorant, we should improve every opportunity of instructing them in the way of salvation. Strive to show them, that man by breaking God's law lost the Divine favor, and that now "God is angry with the wicked every day." Also teach that "God so loved the world, that he gave his only begotten Son, that whosoever believeth on him, might not perish, but have everlasting life."

Tell the sinner of the happiness and blessings which believers in Christ enjoy, both in this life and that which is to come. Also describe to him the extremity and eternity of the torments of the damned; the justice of enduring them for willfully refusing grace; the certainty of death and the judgment; the sinfulness of sin; the preciousness of Christ, and the necessity of regeneration, faith and true holiness.

But be careful in performing this work, to begin with right motives. Do the work with an eye single to the glory of God, and the salvation of men; and also let it be done as quickly as possible. Consider that the sinner stands in a dangerous situation, his time of probation hastening away, and while you may be purposing to save him, sin is taking deeper root, habit is growing strong, the probabilities of his being saved are lessening every hour; temptations to sin multiply; conscience grows seared, the heart hardened,—the devil rules,—Christ is shut out, the Holy Spirit is grieved, God is daily dishonored, his law violated. He is robbed of that glory and service which he should receive, time runs on, death and judgment are at the door, and what if the man die, and drop into hell, while you are purposing to prevent it?

That physician is no better than a murderer, who negligently delays till his patient be dead, or past cure. Go to poor sinners with tears in your eyes, and show them that it is your sense of their danger, and your love to their souls that leads you to speak to them, and warn them to "flee from the wrath to come," and to ask them to consider the solemn question, "How will ye escape, if ye neglect so great a salvation?" And let your manner be serious, and earnest, and labor to make your efforts effectual. Labor to make men know that heaven and hell are not matters to be played with, or to be passed over with a few careless thoughts. Tell them it is most certain, that soon thou shalt be in everlasting joy, or torment; and doth it not awaken thee? Are there so *few* that find the way of life? so many that go the way of death? God is just, and his threatenings are true. Oh friends, what do you think of these things? Alas! it is not a few dull words between jest and earnest, between sleeping and waking, that will rouse a dead hearted sinner. If a house be on fire, you will not make a cold oration on the nature and danger of fire; but will run and cry, "Fire!" "Fire!"

And if we see men in danger of eternal fire, we should not treat them negligently, like as Eli did his sons, but faithfully warn them, so that like the Apostle Paul, we can say, "Wherefore I take you to record this day, that I am pure from the blood of all men." "For I have not shunned to declare unto you all the counsel of God." Acts 20: 26, 27.

In performing this work, we should look up to God for wisdom, and the assistance of his Holy Spirit, to guide us in our efforts, that we may really do as God would have us do. So far as right, I think we should seek out acceptable words, and what we speak should be words of truth. And it is well as much as possible, to have our reproofs and exhortations backed up with the word of God, and to follow sinners with loving, earnest entreaties, and give them no rest in their sins; telling them that the word of the Lord declares, "When the soul hath done that which is lawful and right, and hath kept all my statutes, and done them, he shall surely live." "The soul that sinneth it shall die."

"The son shall not bear the iniquity of the father, neither shall the father bear the iniquity of the son; the righteousness of the righteous shall be upon him, and the wickedness of the wicked shall be upon him." "But if the wicked will turn from all his sins, that he hath committed, and keep all my statutes, and do that which is lawful and right, he shall surely live, he shall not die." "Repent, and turn yourselves from all your transgressions; so iniquity shall not be your ruin." And in the language of the poet we can say,

"There is beyond the sky,
A heaven of joy and love,
And holy children when they die,
Go to that world above.

There is a dreadful hell,
And everlasting pains;
There sinners must with devils dwell,
In darkness, fire and chains."

If Christians earnestly desired the salvation of souls, it would lead them not only to give good counsel, but also to watch for fruit. They should not rest satisfied with a few feeble efforts, but if we have opportunity, "cry aloud and spare not," and show the people their sins. Strive also to save them by your own good example as well as by your words. A faithful consistent Christian life has a great effect in arousing the consciences of sinners around you, and helps greatly to lead them from the path of sin to the service of God.

Let us consider some of the causes why professed Christians do not exert themselves more to save souls. One reason is, because they enjoy so little of God's love in their own hearts. They do not deny themselves as they should, take up their cross and follow Christ. They are guilty of sins they should reprove, and this makes them ashamed to reprove.

Again, there is too much unbelief in men's hearts, concerning God's threatenings to the wicked. He has taught in his holy word that "the wicked shall be turned into hell, with all nations that forget God." But the devil and many of his servants have taught, that the wicked shall not surely die; and have endeavored to make mankind believe in universal salvation. The Bible teaches that "The day is coming in the which all that are in their graves shall hear his voice, and come forth, they that have done good, to the resurrection of life, and they that have done evil, to the resurrection of damnation." Did we *verily believe* that our wicked neighbors and acquaintances, with all that disobey God, except they be converted from the error of their way, and become as little children, they can in no case enter the kingdom of heaven, but "These shall go away into everlasting punishment," did we verily believe this gospel doctrine, would it not lead us to be more zealous in saving our own souls and also the souls of those around us? I think it would. Our efforts to save souls, are much hindered by the want of kind and loving sympathy for those suffering in sin. We see them in their wretchedness, but pass them by, as the priest and levite did by the wounded man. Although the sinner himself does not desire thy help, yet his lost and wretched condition through sin, calls for your sympathy and help. "If God had not heard the cry of our miseries, before he heard the cry of our prayers, and been moved by his own pity before he was moved by our importunity, we might long have continued the slaves of Satan."

You will pray to God for them, to open their eyes, and turn their hearts: and why not endeavor to procure their conversion if you desire it? A sinful, man-pleasing disposition prevents many from laboring for souls as they should. Another reason is a sinful bashfulness. While sinners will swear, get drunk, and neglect the service of God without a blush, we blush when we try to tell them of their sins and endeavor to persuade them from them. "Has not conscience told thee of thy duty many a time, and urged thee to speak to poor sinners; and yet thou hast been ashamed to open thy mouth, and so let them alone to sink or swim." Consider the words of the text, "Whosoever therefore shall be ashamed of me and of my words, in this adulterous and perverse generation, of him also shall the Son of Man be ashamed when he cometh in the glory of his Father, with the holy angels." We need much zeal and patience, and perseverance, if we would convert sinners from the error of their way to the service of Christ.

An idle and impatient spirit hindereth us, for this work does not always succeed at first, except it be followed by patient, persevering, faithful efforts. We must be long in teaching the ignorant, and in persuading the obstinate. We consider not what patience God used toward us when we were in our sins. Wo to us, if God had been as impatient with us as we are with others. And with many, pride is a great hindrance. They do not love to go among the poor and take pains with them in their cottages. "Little know you what many a soul may now be feeling in hell, who died in their sins, for want of your faithful admonition." Think how Christ acted about saving souls, considering them worth the shedding of his blood, so that they might be saved. It is our duty to love our neighbor as ourselves, and do Christians love God with all their hearts, and their neighbor as themselves, that will see their neighbors go on in the broad road to hell and destruction, and never try to hinder them? Consider what a load of guilt it will bring upon thy soul, to neglect this duty! for thou shalt be guilty of the loss of all the souls that perish through your neglect. And if you die unforgiven of your neglected duties, you must perish; and oh, how it will increase your torment to all eternity, to think of souls lost through your neglect, and to see poor souls in torment, and hear them cry out, "oh, if you had but told me plainly of my sin and danger, and set it home to my heart, I might have escaped all this torment." But if you do your duty, you will probably have more joy in heaven the more souls you are instrumental in saving. "Let him know, that he which converteth the sinner from the error of his way, shall save a soul from death, and hide a multitude of sins.'"

Do not despair of success; cannot God give it? And must it not be by means? Do not plead, it will only be casting pearls before swine. When you are in danger to be torn in pieces, Christ would have you forbear; but what is that to you, who are in no such danger? As long as they will hear, you will have encouragement to speak, and may not cast them off as contemptible "swine."

Consider how conscience will trouble you bye and bye, if you continue to neglect this duty. You will remember opportunities when you were in company with the wicked, and had time and fit opportunity to warn them of their sin and danger, and in Christ's stead to persuade them to "flee from the wrath to come," but you did it not, or to little purpose. What a seasonable time you now have for this work. But your neighbors will shortly die, and so will you! Speak to them, therefore, while you may. For if you are faithful in this work, God will have much glory by it, the Church will be multiplied, and your own soul will enjoy more improvement and vigor in the divine life. Be faithful then, even against the greatest discouragements, being "steadfast, unmovable, always abounding in the work of the Lord, forasmuch as ye know that your labor is not in vain in the Lord." For the Lord assists those who come up willingly to do his work. As all Christians have some part of this work to perform, so especially have those whom God in his wisdom has fitted and called to it. A few thoughts to such persons. God especially expects you to work, to whom he has given more learning and knowledge, and endowed with better utterance than your neighbors. God looks for a faithful improvement of your powers and gifts, which if you neglect, it becomes sin; "For to him that knoweth to do good, and doeth it not, to him it is sin." And unless these neglects are forgiven through the atoning merits of Christ, the negligent must perish at last, and others perhaps perish also through their neglect.

And those who are particularly acquainted with some ungodly persons, and have peculiar interest in them; how can you tell but God gave you that interest in them, to this end, that you might be the means of their conversion? Physicians attending the sick, should strive as opportunity affords, to keep a good conscience concerning this duty. You have a peculiar advantage with the ungodly. They look to you with respect, and hope for help, that their bodies may be restored to health, and while you pity their bodily sufferings, and point them to the remedy that may heal them, ah, try to teach them how to live, and how to die, and point them to a remedy for their souls, as you do for their bodies, and try to fit them to enjoy heaven forever. Men of wealth and authority have excellent opportunities for this duty, and may be instrumental in doing much good, if they but have hearts to improve their influence over others. A good man whom God has blessed with wealth, should feel that he is God's steward; and remember that "unto whomsoever much is given, of him shall much be required." If you speak to your neighbors for God, and about their souls, you may be regarded, when even a minister would be despised. As you value the honor of God, your own comfort, and tho salvation of souls, faithfully improve your stewardship, that at last it may be said to you, "Well done, good and faithful servant, enter thou into the joy of thy Lord."

Ministers of the Gospel should make it the main end of all their preaching, praying, studying, and all their labor to glorify God and save souls. They strive with God's help, to "be workmen that need not be ashamed," and work as though they believed the doctrine they taught, even that their hearers must believe and submit to the will of God, and be saved by faith in Christ, or else be lost forever. And those to whom God has entrusted the care of children, let me persuade you to this great work of trying with divine help, to convert and save their souls. Consider what plain and pressing commands of God require this at your hands. "Train up a child in the way he should go, and when he is old he will not depart from it." "Bring up your children in the nurture and admonition of the Lord.' Your care and cost for their bodies will condemn you if you neglect their souls. It is a great charge you are entrusted with, and wo to you if you suffer them to be ignorant or wicked for want of your instruction or correction. But if you succeed in their conversion, and you and they are finally saved, I think it will increase your joy forever to reflect that you tried with the help of grace to do your duty in striving to save their souls. I charge you upon your allegiance to God, and as you will very shortly be brought to the judgment, that you neither refuse nor neglect this important duty. They are with you in their childhood and youth, and may be influenced for good, or evil, easier while young, than when they have become old, even as the young twig can be bent easier than the old oak. If you think you cannot do for them what you would do, still try and do what you can.

Will you resolve now, God willing, that you will enter upon this duty, and neglect it no longer? For the text tells us, "Let him know, that he which converteth the sinner from the error of his way shall save a soul from death, and shall hide a multitude of sins." And if he that converts a sinner from the error of his way, saves a soul from death and hides a multitude of sins, will not all my unconverted readers take the alarm, and try to get converted as soon as possible, that with the help of grace, they may be saved; and also be instrumental in saving souls from death, and hiding a great multitude of sins? As you would not be charged before God as the murderer of souls, nor have them cry out against you in the judgment, see that you teach them to escape it, and bring them up in holiness and the fear of God. If you are not willing to do this work now that you know it to be so great a duty, you are rebels, and no true subjects of Jesus Christ. Try to lead them by your own good example, to prayer, reading God's word, and other religious duties; keep tender their consciences; reform and watch over their outward conversation, and especially observe the Lord's day in this work, and suffer it not to pass away in sports or idleness, but study God's word, and other good books, and recommend the same to others. Keep good company and try to help the ungodly in that way. Try above all, to love and serve God with all your heart, and help others to do so, and then with Divine help, your labor shall not be in vain in the Lord. For He is with those who come up willingly to the help of the Lord.

A LITTLE WORD.

"A little word in kindness spoken,
A motion or a tear
Has often healed the heart that's broken,
And made a friend sincere.

A word—a look—has crushed to earth,
Full many a budding flower,
Which, had a smile but owned its birth,
Would bless life's darkest hour.

Then deem it not an idle thing
A pleasant word to speak,
The face you wear, the thoughts you bring
A heart, may heal or break."

THE HARVEST PAST.

IN reading the book of Jeremiah, we find these words: "*The harvest is past, the summer is ended, and we are not saved.*" Here the prophet speaks in the name of the people, or rather represents them, besieged in Jerusalem, and complaining on account of the length of the siege. Their false prophets had amused them with vain hopes of deliverance, and they had expected the Egyptians to come to their relief. But the harvest went past and the summer came to an end, and no deliverance came to them.

Why was it that they were not saved?

The Bible tells us that the people of Israel forsook the worship of God for that of graven images, and as they provoked him to anger by their idolatries, he would no longer help them. The prophet had seen a vision, in which he had described to him the dreadful calamities and sufferings that were coming on the people, on account of their sins; and he speaks of the thing as already present, because it was soon to happen, and it was represented to him in his vision as already present.

Oh, the great importance of working when it is time to work, and striving to save our souls "while it is called to-day, for soon the night will come, when no man can work."

"Swift the moments fly away,
First the hour, and then the day;
Next the week, the month, the year
Steal away and disappear."

"Now is the accepted time,
The Saviour calls to-day;
To-morrow, it may be too late,
Then why should you delay?"

The people might have repented and forsaken their sins, but they regarded not the word of the Lord: and the harvest went past and the summer ended, and yet they were not saved. "Opportunities are calls from God, they pass by and return no more. Having found what to do, we are required to do it with our might.

This implies at least two things. That we do it without delay, and that we be in good earnest. Many things which our hands find to do at one time, may not be practicable at another; and therefore will not be done at all, if not done immediately.

If we look into the history of the church, we shall find that the men who were the most useful in God's cause, were those who were in real earnest, and who labored with all their might. When God would redeem Israel, it was by one who was prepared to sacrifice a kingdom and a crown in his service, and who esteemed "the reproach of Christ greater riches than the treasures of Egypt."

We are hastening to the grave. Every step we take, every hour we pass, we are going thither. Other things may be uncertain, as whether we are going to heaven or hell; but this is certain, nor do we know how soon we may reach the end of our journey. When we come thither, all our activity for God or man is forever at an end: "for there is no work, nor device, nor knowledge, nor wisdom in the grave whither thou goest." A minister once said at the funeral of a young man, "Whatever he had left undone, was left undone forever." What a loud call then is this to the ungodly. Life is the only time to escape the wrath to come; this time is now in your hand, if you have but a heart to improve it. A door is now open, but soon it will be shut forever. Christ is the way of life and salvation, but the way will be of no use, when we have arrived at the end of our course, and the scene of life is closed up.

What a loud call also to Christians, to redeem the time, and live wholly to the Lord. There is much to do, and the time is short; let us therefore labor with renewed diligence, and be as those who wait for their Lord.

In the days of Noah, God saw that the wickedness of men was great in the earth, and he determined to destroy them by a great flood. But Noah was found righteous before God, and he was commanded to build an ark in which he and his family might be saved. Noah preached righteousness to the people and warned them of the coming flood, but they would not harken to his word, and the "harvest" of opportunity passed, and they were not saved. But as the days of Noah were, so shall also the coming of the Son of Man be. "For as in the days that were before the flood, they were eating and drinking, marrying and giving in marriage, until the day that Noah entered into the ark, and knew not until the flood came, and took them all away; so shall also the coming of the Son of Man be."

"Then shall two be in the field; the one shall be taken and the other left."

"Watch, therefore; for ye know not what hour your Lord doth come. But know this, that if the good man of the house had known in what watch the thief would come, he would have watched, and would not have suffered his house to be broken up."

"Therefore be ye also ready; for in such an hour as ye think not, the Son of Man cometh."

"No room for mirth or trifling here,
For worldly hope or worldly fear,
If life so soon is gone."

"What shall it profit a man if he gain the whole world and lose his own soul?" Its faculties will be lasting as eternity, and to the good I think it will be a source of comfort, to remember, that in their life time they endeavored to do good and keep God's commandments. But it will be a source of sorrow to the wicked, to reflect that they have misimproved their time, their privileges and their talents to the neglect of Christ and his cause. Oh, what a pang went to the rich man's heart when it was told him to "remember, that in his life time he had received his good things, but Lazarus his evil things. Now he is comforted, while thou art tormented."

Let us consider, and strive to make sure work of seeking our own soul's salvation, now while we have time and opportunity. I want my skirts clear, and I would tell you plainly, you cannot go to eternity and say nobody warned me. "No man cared for my soul," but in Scripture language I would say, "surely, I know it shall be well with them that fear God, but it shall not be well with the wicked;" and "what shall it profit a man if he gain the whole world and lose his own soul?" "Remember now thy Creator."

The soul is immortal. In eternity the conscience and memory will not be annihilated. Will a man have an idea of going to heaven blind? No, never. Neither will he go to hell blind. There he shall see the fallen angels; and there he shall have the society of the wicked, and have no comfort forever.

"Fear not them which kill the body but are not able to kill the soul; but rather fear him which is able to destroy both soul and body in hell."

Some, I fear, to whom I now speak, will continue to delay and neglect their souls' salvation, and finally be lost forever.

FUTURE REWARD AND PUNISHMENT.

"*And it came to pass that the beggar died and was carried by the angels into Aaraham's bosom; the rich man also died and was buried; and in hell he lifted up his eyes, being in torments, and seeth Abraham afar off, and Lazarus in his bosom.*" Luke 16: 22, 23.

I wish to call your attention to four leading ideas contained in these verses: which are, 1st, The fact noticed, the two men spoken of, both died. 2d, Their condition before they died. 3d, Their condition after death. 4th, The inducements held out to us, to escape hell and get to heaven.

Let us look at the first thought. The two men spoken of both died. In the Bible it says, "It is appointed unto men once to die, and after death the judgment." The rich, the poor, the middle class, the good and bad, men of all conditions in life; it is appointed unto all once to die. We can none of us escape it. With the exception of only two men, Enoch and Elijah, very holy men, who walked with God, keeping his commandments, and were taken home to heaven without suffering death; with these two exceptions, all the thousands who have lived before us have died. Yes, and we are passing away. Death is on our track. Soon we shall be calle l to die. Out of the thousands who have lived, there probably is not one now living that is two hundred years old. It is supposed from accounts that we receive, that one dies every second. That would be sixty every minute, or thirty-six hundred every hour. Truly, whate'er we do, where'er we are, we are traveling to the tomb. 2d. Consider the condition of those two men before they died. It is said of one, "he was rich." This in Christ's account is the first part of his sin. "Here is the first degree of his reprobation, he got all he could, and kept all to himself. He did not devote it to the glory of God. It is not considered a sin to have an abundance of this world's goods, but it is a sin to become proud of what God has given us, and not to devote it to his service. The second part of his sin, he was clothed with purple and fine linen. Thirdly, he fared sumptuously every day. And Adam Clark says in his comment on this passage of Scripture, "That no other evil is spoken of him, and in comparison with thousands, he was not only blameless, but he was a virtuous man." "And considering all the circumstances, our blessed Lord does not represent this man as a monster of inhumanity; but merely as an indolent man, who sought and had his portion in this life, and was not at all concerned about any other;" and Christ has said, "a man cannot serve two masters."

Now consider the condition of the other man. It is stated in the verse, "There was a certain beggar, which was laid at his" (the rich man's) "gate, full of sores." It seems then, that he was poor and afflicted. Yet Dr. Clark tells us, "his character was good." And if so, he was a happy man, with all his afflictions. The Bible tells us, "Happy is the man whose God is the Lord." "The fear of the Lord is the beginning of wisdom." "Her ways are ways of pleasantness, and all her paths are peace." The poet says,

"How happy every child of grace,
Who knows his sins forgiven;
This earth, he cries, is not my place,
I seek my place in heaven."

This brings us to the third part of our subject. Their condition after death! 1st, In the verse it says, "And it came to pass that the beggar died, and was carried by the angels into Abraham's bosom." This was a phrase used by the Jews, to signify "the Paradise of God." The end of Lazarus was glorious. Although he was poor and afflicted when on earth, yet he feared God, and when death came he was not left alone; for a company of angels were sent, which brought him safely home to heaven. Glory be to God. "Mark the perfect man, and behold the upright, for the end thereof is peace." 2d. The "rich man also died, and was buried, and in hell he lifted up his eyes, being in torments." Look at the circumstances of his punishment. First, He sees Lazarus in heaven, clothed with glory and immortality. Second, as stated in the 25th verse, he was told by Abraham to remember that in his life time he received his good things. We are to remember if lost in hell, that we have had time, grace and opportunities to prepare for heaven, and that it is our own fault that we are lost. But unless we repent of our sins, there is no escaping it. Jesus said, except ye repent ye shall all likewise perish. Sinners will die and go to hell, unless they repent, get converted, and are reconciled to God when they die. Third circumstance, "Actual torments in the flames of the bottomless pit, will form through all eternity, a continual source of indescribable wo. Fourth circumstance, There will be an eternal desire to escape evil, and an eternal desire to get to heaven, which it is impossible for those to do who once go down to hell. The prisoners in jail and many other places of confinement may look forward to the time of their release with a kind of joy. But not so with those shut up in the prison of hell. "The smoke of their torment ascendeth up forever and ever."

The difference in the conditions of these two men after

death is simply this; the one though poor in this world, in the general acceptation, was taken at death by angels up to heaven, there to enjoy an eternity of happiness. While the rich man who felt that it was not his business to trouble himself about serving God here, found himself after death in hell, there to wail and weep, and be tormented in the flames of fire through all eternity.

We come now to the 4th part of our subject, and let us consider the inducements held out to us to escape hell, and get to heaven. Jesus said, "It were better to lose one eye, than having two eyes to be cast into hell, where the worm dieth not, and the fire is not quenched." Also, "Lay up for yourselves treasures in heaven, where neither moth nor rust doth corrupt, nor thieves break through and steal." Heaven is a safe place to put our treasures in, and we shall be rewarded in eternity, according to our works here.

Reasons why we should wish to escape hell.

1st. The wicked will be there as our companions.

2d. The smoke of their torment will ascend up forever.

3d. Annihilation of either body or soul will never take place in hell. The meaning of annihilation is, reducing to nothing, ceasing to exist. Some believe, or say so at least, that when we die, that is the end of us; but that is not the fact. For we shall all live again, at the time of the resurrection. "Those who have done good shall come forth to the resurrection of life, and those who have done evil, to the resurrection of damnation." Our memory, our conscience, and devils, and the lost souls of men, who have been our neighbors here, and have been brought down to perdition through our influence, will never cease to exist. but will be there, as sources of torment and unhappiness to us.

Now look at the inducements placed before us to lead

us to heaven. 1st. There will be nothing there to hurt us. The weather will be neither too cold nor too hot, but will be comfortable for us. And God shall wipe away all tears from their eyes, and there shall be no more death nor separation of friends, nor sorrow, nor crying; for the former things are passed away.

2d. We shall there have the company of Jesus our Saviour, and the holy angels, and all the good Christians who have overcome Satan and all his works, and having been faithful until death, have received a crown of life.

3d. We shall there be clothed in garments of white and spotless purity.

4th. There will be no night there.

5th. There will be no tempting devil there to tempt us to sin. There the wicked will be excluded, and nothing can enter there that can injure or make afraid. Read what is written of heaven's inhabitants, in Rev. 7: 9–17. "After this I beheld, and lo, a great multitude, which no man could number, of all nations, and kindreds, and people and tongues, stood before the throne, and before the Lamb, clothed with white robes, and palms in their hands; and cried with a loud voice, saying, Salvation to our God which sitteth on the throne, and unto the Lamb. And all the angels stood round about the throne, and about the elders and the four beasts, and fell before the throne on their faces, and worshiped God, saying, Amen; blessing and glory, and wisdom, and thanksgiving, and honor, and power, and might, be unto our God forever and ever. Amen. And one of the elders answered, saying unto me, What are these which are arrayed in white robes? and whence came they? And I said unto him, Sir, thou knowest. And he said to me, These are they which came out of great tribulation, and have washed their robes, and made them white in the blood of the Lamb. Therefore are they before the throne of God, and serve him day and night in his temple; and he that sitteth on the throne shall dwell among them. They shall hunger no more, neither thirst any more; neither shall the sun light on them, nor any heat. For the Lamb, which is in the midst of the throne, shall feed them, and shall lead them unto living fountains of waters; and God shall wipe away all tears from their eyes."

Now as heaven, with all its joys and pleasures, is inviting us to come in; and hell with all its terrors, is warning us to keep out, let us be reconciled to God.

Here read what is written in Rev. 22: 12–18. "And, behold, I come quickly; and my reward is with me, to give every man as his work shall be.

I am Alpha and Omega, the beginning and the end, the first and the last. Blessed are they that do his commandments, that they may have right to the tree of life, and may enter in through the gates into the city. For without are dogs, and sorcerers, and whoremongers, and murderers, and idolators, and whosoever loveth and maketh a lie.

I Jesus have sent mine angel to testify unto you these things in the churches. I am the root and offspring of David, and the bright and morning star.

And the Spirit and the Bride say, Come. And let him that heareth say, Come. And let him that is athirst come. And whosoever will, let him take of the water of life freely."

THOUGHTS ON TEMPERANCE.

"*Who hath wo? who hath sorrow? who hath contentions? who hath babbling? who hath wounds without cause? who hath redness of eyes? They that tarry long at the wine. Look not thou upon the wine when it is red, when it giveth his color in the cup, when it moveth itself aright: At the last it biteth like a serpent, and stingeth like an adder.*" Prov. 23: 29–32.

I once knew a young man, who was in the habit of drinking intoxicating drinks. I spoke to him kindly, and I think I warned him of his danger. He looked up with a smile and spoke as though I need not fear about him. But within a few weeks from that time, he was found dead, and it was supposed, that, while he was intoxicated, he had fallen from a piazza and broken his neck. "Wherefore, let him that thinketh he standeth take heed lest he fall." "At the last it biteth like a serpent, and stingeth like an adder.'"

In speaking of social drinking, an author says: "Intemperance does not come at once, with its burning streams to consume the heart of its victim, but slowly and gradually it drags itself along, taking one fortress after another, until the fashionable, genteel, moderate drinker has become the reeling, bloated, degraded drunkard."

There is something in the idea of taking a social glass with a friend, or drinking a cup of sparkling wine on some public occasion, exceedingly pleasant. The young fail to perceive the danger of the practice. They cannot see how it is, that a man is led on from moderation, to brutal excess, and hence they use the wine-cup freely, and without fear of any evil consequences. The idea that he shall become a drunkard, does not enter into the mind of the young man when first he sips the poison. And thus it has ever been with those who have become intemperate.

Step by step the habit grew upon him; deeper and deeper he descended into the vortex of wretchedness, until the last lamp which shed its light upon his path was put out, the last star of hope sank in darkness.

I am perhaps addressing those who occasionally make use of intoxicating drinks, and who, on social occasions deem it well to take the cup of wine, without hesitation. You do not perceive any signs of danger, and should one remonstrate with you personally, you would consider it an insult. "Can I not govern myself?" you would ask, with outraged feelings. "Can I not drink when I please, and let it alone when I please?" "Have I no power over my appetite and passions?" The same questions others have asked, and yet have been hurried into the whirlpool of drunkenness. Others when remonstrated with, have been as indignant as yourself, but have ultimately found, that the cup was poison, that *death lurked beneath its brim*, that the deathless worm was coiled up there, that it burned the soul with deathless flame.

I have read of a man who kept a tiger in his house. He had secured the animal when it was quite young, and by kindness and gentleness, had apparently subdued its ferocious and bloodthirsty disposition. So attached to his pet did he become, that he took the creature to bed with him at night, and let it follow him in his travels. Friends remonstrated, and urged the nature of the animal, and predicted danger. The foolish man laughed at their fear, and ridiculed the idea of danger. At length he went to s'eep at night as usual with the beast by his side. Turning in his bed, he drew his hand across one of the paws of his favorite. The wound streamed with blood. The tiger tasted it. His ferocious nature, which had been curbed for years, was aroused, and when the morning came, all that remained of his master was a bleeding, mangled corpse.

The man who sports with intemperance in any form, who drinks moderately, or immoderately, is tampering with the tiger. He will realize the truth of Scripture, "At the last it biteth like a serpent, and stingeth like an adder." And further, the scriptures tell us, "Know ye not, that the unrighteous shall not inherit the kingdom of God? Be not deceived: neither fornicators, nor idolators, nor thieves, nor covetous, nor *drunkards* shall inherit the kingdom of God." 1 Cor. 6 : 9-10.

Let us now consider what is intemperance? According to Webster, "Intemperance is 1st, In a general sense, want of moderation, or due restraint; excess in any kind of action, or indulgence.

2d. Habitual indulgence in drinking spirituous liquors, with or without intoxication." Business once called me into a store, and there I saw a man of my acquaintance. I had been told a few days before, that he had had the delirium tremens. While I was in the store, I saw him ask hurriedly for a glass of liquor. The glass and the decanter were set before him. He filled the glass nearly full of liquor, and without water or sugar, he poured it down his throat, as though he thought his life depended on swallowing it in the quickest possible time. That, I think was intemperance.

I have read that "men of genius are often unfortunately addicted to drinking. There is a melancholy which is apt to come like a cloud over the imaginations of such characters. To relieve these feelings, many plans have been adopted." I have also read, that Dr. Johnson fled for years to wine under his habitual gloom. He found that the pangs were removed while its immediate influence lasted, but he also found that they returned with double force, when that influence passed away. He saw the dangerous precipice on which he stood, and by a determined effort he gave it over.

Let us consider some of the results of intemperance. "Intemperance ruins the physical constitution." In the creation of the body, God has displayed infinite wisdom. More wonderful than any complicated work of human hands, it bears the impress of divinity. It is fearfully and wonderfully made, and is a specimen of workmanship, unrivaled in the arts. The Maker of man did not form him thus fearfully, in order that he might be broken by disease, and crushed by vice. He made him upright. He stamped the blush of health upon his cheek, and sent him forth to look upon the earth beneath his feet, and the heavens above his head.

"You have seen a beautiful machine, fulfilling the purpose of its maker, and working with order, regularity and harmony. You have examined it closely, and admired the perfection of all its parts. You have complimented the skill of the artizan, and deemed his work one of extraordinary ingenuity. You have also seen that machine disarranged; the order and harmony of its movements gone, and entirely incapable of performing the work for which the maker designed it." "The human body under the influence of intemperance, is like that disarranged and broken instrument. The purpose of its creation is defeated, and it becomes the seat of numberless diseases, aches and pains, sorrows and woes, for which God never has intended it. The drunkard presents a fearful specimen of a broken down man. From the head to the feet he is covered with disease. He moves along the street, with downcast eyes, or staggers to and fro, with heavy tread; his nerves are all unstrung, or braced beyond endurance; his head aches and throbs; his bloated face spoils the beauty of a human being; his knees totter and smite against each other; his livid lips are closed over teeth decayed; his swollen tongue prevents his ready utterance; his idiotic look betokens speedy death; his eye glares at one time, and is languid and bloodshot at another; and his brain is racked with a thousand fancies, and agonized by a thousand fears. Go, search earth's darkest caves, and bring up to the blaze of day, the inmates of your prisons and dungeons; your insane asylums and madhouses, and none will you find so miserable and degraded, so lost to all that makes up a perfect man, as the victim of intemperance.

Take some case within the limits of your own observation; some friend who tampered with the terrible destroyer, and has been ruined. You knew him perhaps, when no shade of crime had passed over his manly countenance; when he walked with his head erect, and his bosom bared to the storms of life; when life flashed from his eye, and vigor was in his step; when the stranger noted his manly form, and correct deportment. You have seen that form bend, not with age; you have seen that step falter, not from fear, and that once noble form, reeling from the drunkard's purgatory, to lie besotted and beast-like by the wayside. You have seen every thing noble and beautiful in this God-made body, utterly spoiled. The divinity in man crushed out of him, and the temple of the immortal soul laid in ruins. Nor will the young men whom I address avoid this terrible destruction of the human system, if they enter the fatal avenues which lead to the drunkard's fate. They may suppose that they have power to drink, or refrain from drinking. They may boast how strong they are, and how easily they can dash the inebriating cup to the earth. But their boasts are idle as the wind. The great

The Victim of Intemperance.

army of drunkards, with crippled limbs, limping forms, bleeding hearts, and maddened brain, thousands of whom die every year, utter their notes of warning. The broken, diseased, death-struck forms of prostrate men, as they lie along the path of life, give fearful admonition. The opening graves, into which the remains of men are tumbled after they have cursed themselves and all around them; graves on which the flowers seem unwilling to bloom, and over which the birds appear to sing in sadness; graves wet by no widow's tears, consecrated by no orphan's lament; graves which angels shun, or by which they weep in sorrow, as on their mission of mercy, they pass through the city of the dead, all sound the alarm, and by the dumb eloquence of their speechless harmony, bid the living throng beware of the drunkard's hopeless doom. You may perhaps have heard of the famous dream or vision of a distinguished clergyman, for the publication of which he was beaten in the street and imprisoned. The scene was said to be in Deacon Giles' Distillery. The dreamer saw the demon-workmen at their unhallowed employment, manufacturing with great zeal the elixir of death. He heard their ferocious and blasphemous expressions. While he gazed on, barrel after barrel of the accursed poison was drawn from the cistern, and prepared for sale. The employment of one or more of the fiends was to mark and label these barrels and hogsheads of rum and gin, which had been put up. Quenching a coal of fire in the liquid which he had made, the infernal monster went to work. On all the barrels, in letters which would remain invisible until the first glass was drawn, and then burn forth like fire, he wrote, "consumption," "palsy," "fever," "plague," "insanity," "madness," "redness of eyes," "sorrow of heart," "death," "damnation," and the like expressions, which when the liquid deaths had been sold, and the buyers drew from it for the first time, flashed out in the faces of the thirsty customers, who stood waiting at the bar. With fearful consternation they saw written in words of flame, the diseases which they knew were praying upon their systems, and fled from the place in terror.

What that dreamer saw in vision, we behold as an existing fact. Though on the barrels in the rum-shops, we do not find the words of fire written there by demon hands, yet we behold more fearful inscriptions on the living, dying countenances of men who walk our streets. Gleaming forth from fiery eyes; seen on the wan and haggard cheek; read in the stooping forms and staggering tread; heard in the hollow cough; felt in the aching head, and beating heart, proving to us that intemperance

> "Is palsy, plague and fever,
> And madness, all combined."

THEY ALL DRINK WATER.

Pinks with white and crimson streaks,
On their soft and dimpled cheeks;
Sweet violets whose azure eyes,
Won their beauty from the skies;
Dear daisies touched with silver sheen,
Shining on hill and valleys green,
And dandelions crowned with gold,
Drink only water pure and cold.
Sparrows at our thresholds fed,
Robins with their bosoms red,
Meadow-larks in fields of green,
Orioles that light the scene.
Bluebirds with their coats of blue,
Blackbirds of the sable-hue,
And the jolly bobolink,
From the springs and streamlets drink.
Mary, whose eyes are soft and blue,
Sarah, whose cheeks have a crimson hue,
Jane, whose teeth are white as pearls,
Susie, whose hair rolls down in curls,
Katie, whose brow is broad and fair,
Emma, whose face is free of care,
And Lizzie, the merchant's daughter,
Drink only water, water, water!

Youth's Temperance Banner.

INDEX.

www.ingramcontent.com/pod-product-compliance
Lightning Source LLC
Chambersburg PA
CBHW022153090426
42742CB00010B/1495

* 9 7 8 3 3 3 7 8 7 7 0 2 6 *